# BIG

## TAKE YOUR LIFE FROM ORDINARY TO EXTRAORDINARY.

### @ScottWilliams

I WOULD LIKE TO THANK GOD, MY FAMILY AND EVERYONE
ELSE WHO HAS CHALLENGED ME TO GO BIG.

2410 W. Memorial Rd.
Suite C #260
Oklahoma City, OK 73134

nxtlevel.net

ISBN: 978-0-9882096-0-2
Printed in the United States of America
Library of Congress Cataloging-in-Publication Data

For information regarding author interviews or speaking engagements, please contact the public relations department – PR@nxtlevel.net

## Go BIG

TABLE OF CONTENTS

---

## Take Your Life From Ordinary To Extraordinary

# OR·DI·NAR·Y

AWR-DN-ER-EE
*adjective, noun.*

1. of no special quality or interest; commonplace; unexceptional:

2. plain or undistinguished: ordinary clothes.

3. somewhat inferior or below average; mediocre.

4. customary; usual; normal.

# EX·TRAOR·DI·NAR·Y

IK-STRAWR-DN-ER-EE, EK-STRUH-AWR-
*adjective.*

1. beyond what is usual, ordinary, regular, or established:

2. exceptional in character, amount, extent, degree, etc.;

noteworthy; remarkable:

# THIS YEAR IS GOING TO BE BETTER THAN THE LAST

**T**his year is going to be better than the last. How many times have you told yourself that at the start of a new year? It feels great to make plans and think positive about having an amazing, impressive, magnificent, astonishing or [insert adjective of choice] type of year.

**"The reality is that this year will be no different than any other year without the 3-F's: Faith, Focus and Follow-Through."**

On New Year's Day 2012, I tweeted the above statement about Faith, Focus and Follow-through, and I received several replies from people quoting and making reference to Christian athlete and All-Pro NFL receiver Larry Fitzgerald. After doing a little research, I found that Larry's motto is "Faith, Focus, Finish."

There are a number of ways to iterate the slogan, such as "Faith, Focus, Fulfill" or "Faith, Focus, Finalize." No matter how you slice it, the key elements of it are 1) having faith first, and then 2) staying focused, followed by 3) ensuring the goals are completed.

The 3-F's allow us to embrace the ultimate truth that successful plans are God-centered and able to be accomplished no matter when you start living them out. Every day is the beginning of a new year, whether it's January or July. Start now and make the next 12 months a huge success!

*"Mortals make elaborate plans, but God has the last word. Humans are satisfied with whatever looks good; God probes for what is good. Put God in charge of your work, then what you've planned will take place. God made everything with a place and purpose ... "* Proverbs 16:1-4 MSG.

You have a place and purpose on this earth. You were created to succeed at what you do, and to help others succeed. You were made to be a conqueror, not to be defeated. You were made so that every work started in you shall be completed. You were built in a manner that no weapon formed against you shall prosper. You were made for more than haphazardly getting through this year. With Faith, Focus and Follow-through, this year will be different, you will be different, your family will be different, and those around you will be different. Get ready to Go BIG… get ready to move your life from ordinary to extraordinary.

Cheers to a successful year!

*"Most people give up just when they're about to achieve success. They quit on the one-yard line. They give up at the last minute of the game, one foot from a winning touchdown."* ~ Ross Perot

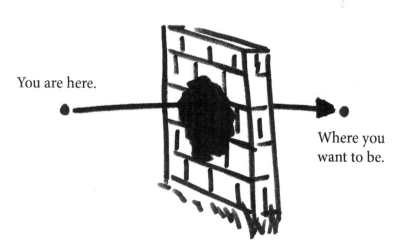

You are here.

Where you want to be.

FAITH, FOCUS, FOLLOW-THROUGH

Fear is one of the most common inhibitors, keeping people from moving toward what they want to be. Fear keeps people's lives ordinary, while their hearts burn with longing for the extraordinary thing they were made for.

The 3-F's will help you break through the fear barrier. They'll help you understand that God wants you to achieve the extraordinary, and that He has not given you the spirit of fear.

The key is to reinforce the 3-F's in your daily life. And that's the purpose of this book. By following seven simple lessons, and adjusting them to create a daily practice that works for you, you'll not only get where you want to be... you'll get higher and farther than you could imagine.

As an added bonus, the end of each chapter contains three elements to help you GO DEEPER into the concepts and principles discussed in each chapter.

The Go DREAM section will help you think about the kind of faith you need to accomplish the dreams God put inside you. This section includes questions to get you thinking differently about yourself, others and God.

The Go DIG section is designed to help you interact with what God says about the subject matter in each chapter. Learning to focus on what God says about each concept will give you the confidence and courage to begin doing what He instructs you to do.

The Go DO section guides you in putting the concepts and principles into practice. Faith and focus without follow-through are dead. We need to learn what it truly means to be a doer of the Word and not just hearers (or in this case, not just readers).

Let's Go BIG!

DON'T SET OUT TO DO EXTRAORDINARY THINGS; RATHER, ORDINARY THINGS IN AN EXTRAORDINARY MANNER.

**TAKE YOUR LIFE FROM ORDINARY TO EXTRAORDINARY.**

CHECK
YOUR
REARVIEW
MIRROR

## CHAPTER 1

## CHECK YOUR REARVIEW MIRROR

> "Losers live in the past. Winners learn from the past and enjoy working in the present toward the future."
>
> DENIS WAITLEY

**W**hen you're on your way somewhere, direction is everything. That's why most of us rely on our GPS to get us where we need to go. If we get off track or miss an exit, we expect our GPS to "recalculate," help us make a proper U-turn and point us in a new direction. Bottom line is we don't care how we get there; we just want to get there in a timely manner.

To get to an extraordinary tomorrow, we have take a look back at where we've been. I'm not encouraging you to live in the past or dwell on yesterday's mistakes. I'm also not encouraging you to survive and thrive on yesterday's successes. I am encouraging you to take a look back at the previous year and reflect on your successes, failures and what stayed the same. Make your necessary recalculations and keep moving forward on your journey of success.

Believe me, I know it's difficult to re-calculate and evaluate yourself honestly. That's why it's important to have people close to you, who can give you honest feedback. I have several mentors that I not only give permission to speak into my life, but also seek their opinion in order to recalibrate. Outside of my mentors, my wife, children, close friends and family speak very candidly to me and give honest feedback. Often, those closest to you are great resources - They don't just know you well; they generally have your best interests at heart.

Once you begin asking yourself the tough questions about last year, the scariest part is out of the way. With the guilt, shame and past failures discarded, you're positioned to make something happen.

Purposefully examining the past, with a focus on how it connects to the present, puts you on the path to better results in the future. A great approach to looking at the past and focusing on a successful future is an old method I always used for project management, known as SSCC--Stop, Start, Continue and Change. See chart on the next page.

I love thinking of New Year strategy or strategy in general as a rearview mirror. A rearview mirror has a simple function: to help you see what's behind you. It also gives you some perspective as to what's coming up beside you. A friend of mine who's licensed to drive a big rig says that drivers are taught to always check all of their mirrors to make sure they know what's going on around them.

Of course, focusing only on what's in your rearview mirror will land you in a ditch pretty quickly. Your primary responsibility when driving, and in life, is to pay attention to what's ahead.

What's ahead is the achievement of the God-sized goals and God-sized vision placed in front of you. Go Big!

*"Friends, don't get me wrong: By no means do I count myself an expert in all of this, but I've got my eye on the goal, where God is beckoning us onward-to Jesus. I'm off and running, and I'm not turning back. So let's keep focused on that goal, those of us who want everything God has for us. If any of you have something else in mind, something less than total commitment, God will clear your blurred vision - you'll see it yet! Now that we're on the right track, let's stay on it." Philippians 3:13-16*

# STOP, START, CONTINUE, CHANGE

## STOP

What did you do last year that didn't work?

_____

_____

_____

_____

What are you currently doing that you need to STOP?

_____

_____

_____

_____

## START

What are some things that you didn't do last year that you should have?

_____

_____

_____

_____

What do you need to START doing?

_____

_____

_____

_____

# CONTINUE

What did you do last year that worked?

_____

_____

_____

What things worked last year that you are going to continue to do?

_____

_____

_____

# CHANGE

What things had potential last year?

_____

_____

_____

What things can benefit from minor tweaks, attention and changes?

_____

_____

_____

_____

# GET YOUR PRIORITIES STRAIGHT

As I travel, speak, consult and mentor individuals worldwide, it seems as though I'm always in conversations with people who are operating from a mindset of "Where do I go from here?" Nine times out of ten, the conversation centers around what they're doing professionally, what God has called them to do, and the amount of time they spend with their family. They all have one thing in common—struggle. They struggle with putting people and success over family, putting their job over their marriage, and putting their drive for success over their kids.

No matter what dreams God has given us, there will always be tension as we struggle with "getting our priorities straight." I sometimes receive Twitter, Facebook and email notes from people who have observed, via my online status updates, the way my wife LaKendria and I interact with our sons. It may be comments about something as simple as the weekly visits my sons and I make to Sonic Drive-In and the barbershop. I usually tweet about our weekly flavored drink experiences (cherry-limeades, cranberry-vanilla-sprites, vanilla-Cokes, pineapple-vanilla-sprites, Ocean Water... for all you Sonic regulars) and the barbershop talk of the day. I try to talk write about the seemingly ordinary moments in our everyday life.

I remember one sweltering Saturday afternoon when my wife and I were at our son's track meet in Texas. Did I mention that it was "Texas hot"? That's hot plus 10 degrees. While I was sitting under a tent between events, I checked my phone and read an email that made me think about priorities and purpose from someone commenting on my tweets: *"Scott, your care for your children is the bomb! I don't often see folks so willing to tote their children so many places when they're involved in so many extracurricular activities. You're a great example."*

Notes like that always remind me of the simple fact that our focus and follow-through are dictated by our priorities. This email was an indicator that I'd been choosing my priorities wisely. I'm not saying everyone's week must involve Sonic runs or being involved in lots of extracurricular activities. Your priorities are different than mine. But whatever we do, we must be purposeful in matching the time we spend to the things we believe are most important. That's why this chapter could just as easily be titled "Focus on the Things That Matter," or "Your Family is More Important Than Your Desire to Take Care of Your Family."

As we go about our busy days, filled with many activities, choices, options, decisions and distractions, we must ask ourselves this simple question: **"What's the Purpose?"** If the answer to that question is lame or selfish, or if you find yourself making up an answer, or if you can't come up with an answer at all, it's time to do something different and reset your direction. Think about the people and situations of your life and intentionally ask yourself these questions:

**What's The Purpose?**

- What's the purpose of this relationship?
- What's the purpose of the sinful behavior?
- What's the purpose of how I spend my time and money?
- What's the purpose of spending more time at work than with my family?
- What's the purpose of a work promotion that constitutes a demotion of my family?
- What's the purpose of all the personality morphing I go through just to be well-liked in different environments?
- What's the purpose of talking about what I want to do instead of doing it?
- What's the purpose in having another drink?
- What's the purpose in always pointing out what others are doing wrong?
- What's the purpose of what I'm doing today?
- What's the purpose of what I plan on doing tomorrow?
- What's the purpose? What's the purpose? What's the purpose?

500 years ago, Thomas à Kempis said this: *"Life without a purpose is a languid drifting thing; every day we ought to review our purpose,*

*saying to ourselves, 'This day let me make a sound beginning, for what we have hitherto done is naught.'"*

Let's do this!

"Action expresses priorities."

MAHATMA GANDHI

## GO DREAM

1. What direction do you think you're heading right now?

☐ DRIVING TOWARDS GOD?

☐ REVERSING AWAY FROM GOD?

☐ STUCK IN NEUTRAL?

2. If you could be on the exact road to lead you where you want to go, what would be the name of the road? Pastor Place? Doctor Drive? Astronaut Alley? Lover's Lane? Consultant Court? Take a moment and write down the name of your dream road.

_____   ☐ ALY ☐ CR ☐ DR ☐ PL
                                   ☐ AVE ☐ CT ☐ LN ☐ RD

3. If you were to ask your top five friends, "Do you think I'm heading in the right direction," what would they say?

1. _____   _____
   NAME                   RESPONSE
2. _____   _____
   NAME                   RESPONSE
3. _____   _____
   NAME                   RESPONSE
4. _____   _____
   NAME                   RESPONSE
5. _____   _____
   NAME                   RESPONSE

4. What's keeping you from pushing the gas and taking the trip of your life?

_____

_____

# GO DIG

1. Read Isaiah 48:17: *This is what the LORD says—your Redeemer, the Holy One of Israel: "I am the LORD your God, who teaches you what is best for you, who directs you in the way you should go."*

Do you believe that God has your best interest in mind? Are you allowing him to direct you? Does your street name match His street name for you?

_____

_____

_____

_____

_____

2. Read Philippians 3:13-16. *"Friends, don't get me wrong: By no means, do I count myself an expert in all of this, but I've got my eye on the goal, where God is beckoning us onward to Jesus. I'm off and running, and I'm not turning back. So let's keep focused on that goal, those of us who want everything God has for us. If any of you have something else in mind, something less than total commitment, God will clear your blurred vision - you'll see it yet! Now that we're on the right track, let's stay on it."*

Do you know what the goal is? If so, do you have your eye on it? Are you totally committed to the goal Paul talks about?

_____

_____

_____

_____

_____

3. Read Psalms 17:5. *"My steps have held to your path, my feet have not stumbled."*

Is this statement true of you? Are you walking/driving on the path that God desires for you, or are you stumbling around on your own path?

_____

_____

_____

# GO DO

1. Make a road sign of the path that you need to be on. Be creative. Get out the crayons and markers and be a kid again! Put it on the refrigerator so you can see it every the morning. Let this road sign feed your soul!

**Bonus!** Go ask five of your friends if they believe you're on the right path. Ask them to be honest with you. Ask them if they believe that you're currently reaching your potential. Ask them to pray for you. Friends don't let friends drive alone!

# NOTES

_____
_____
_____
_____
_____
_____
_____
_____
_____
_____
_____
_____
_____
_____
_____

## ACTION ITEMS

- [ ] 
- [ ] 
- [ ] 
- [ ] 

## THOUGHTS

- [ ] 
- [ ] 
- [ ] 
- [ ]

# THREE SPHERES OF FOCUS

## CHAPTER 2

---

## THREE SPHERES OF FOCUS

---

> *"Many men go fishing all of their lives without knowing it is not fish they are after."*
>
> HENRY DAVID THOREAU

etting your priorities straight consists of getting the following three things in the right order and from the right context. I call these the **Three Spheres of Focus.** (see diagram on previous page) Think of them as concentric circles, starting with God at the center, growing outward to encompass the farthest reaches of your life.

**1. God** – This is where you begin, and it's pretty simple. Love God, seek God, worship God, study God's Word, spend time with God, pray, seek, give, listen, read and strive for your God-given potential. Jesus makes it plain in Luke 9:23: *"Then He said to them all: 'Whoever wants to be my disciple must deny themselves and take up their cross daily and follow me.'"*

Following God isn't automatic; it's a daily choice for each of us. It involves the willing submission of your desires and will to His desires and will. For God to be a genuine priority, He has to come before all others. Pick a time and place to spend with God and don't let anything get in the way of your daily time with Him.

Another important way to put God first is in your finances. One of the best books I've read about this area is *The Blessed Life* by Robert Morris, the pastor of Gateway Church (several locations in the Dallas, TX metro area.) He's the author of many great books. In *The Blessed Life*, he offers the simple secret to achieving guaranteed financial results. Instead of writing about it, I'll simply encourage you to pick up a copy of the book; it has blessed my family, and it will bless yours as well.

**2. Family** – Invest in your family, invest in your marriage, invest in your kids and put family above everything else besides God.

Most likely, you already consider your family more important than your image, work, status, etc. But even the most loving parents can let their sense of responsibility get ahead of actual time with the family. It's critical to realize *that your family is more important than your desire to take care of your family.* Don't put the latter before the former.

If you talk to anyone that has lost someone they loved, they will always talk about the **moments** and **memories** that they had with that person. The same thing is true for the parents that look back and remember when their children were toddlers.

Each moment is a precious gift from God, filled with extraordinary potential if we only take the time to savor it. Think about your child's first step, piano recital, gymnastics meet, their decision to follow Christ, football games, challenging times, reciting Scripture/memory verses together, open house at school, trick or treating, college graduation, their wedding day and beyond.

Create some **non-negotiables** for you and your family–a family night, a game night, date nights, phone/Internet and "TV time" rules. Find the non-negotiables that will make the biggest difference for your family, and make sure they are upheld. Whatever they are, frame your decisions with these two questions: *Are the things I'm doing in today's moments creating the right family memories for tomorrow? Am I finding fulfillment even in the little moments God provides?*

One of the best non-negotiables for married couples, with or without children, is a date night. As a pastor, I have married many couples over the years, and a date night is the one thing that I tell them is non-negotiable (aside from putting God first in the relationship). My wife and I facilitated a Prep For Marriage class at church several times a year over a five-year period. We saw well over a hundred couples in those years, and we told each of them the same thing. A date night is simple, and it's defined as any period of time a husband and wife set aside to spend quality time together without the kids.

Date nights are not only good for the couple, but also a great example for kids who see their parents dating one another. Early on, my youngest son Jayden asked me, "Dad, why are you taking mom on a date and you're already married to her?" I chuckled, recognizing a "teachable moment." I responded, "Because your mom and I are married and I love her dearly. I'm going to always take her on a date … I expect you to do the same when you're older and get married." Jayden smiled from ear to ear. LaKendria and I continue to have date nights.

There are many different options for date nights. What you do is not as important as the fact that you make sure the activities and time together are designated as a date night. It's important to remember that this is a date, a break from the monotony of everyday life. This is a time to focus on each other. The frequency of date night depends on the couple; the range is anywhere from weekly to monthly, but no less than once a month.

Every day is an opportunity to create special moments and memories with your family. It's important to remember that if you're going to have a successful year, you have to embrace the precious moments and memories as they happen. Don't wait until you've got time to enjoy these moments—enjoy them now.

**3. Everything Else** – After God and family, everyone has different priorities. It's important to sit down as a family and figure out what those priorities are. Some people may think my family's priorities are jacked up, because we spend so much time "toting our kids around," as the person said in the email I referred to earlier. It's a framework that works for us, but may not work for you. We have found it to be a huge blessing to travel every weekend in the summer for track meets. They create an opportunity for us to pack up our cooler with lunch, snacks and goodies, and basically have a family picnic sprinkled with a little competition every weekend. Let's thank God for the freedom to choose how to follow the unique callings He gives each of us.

Even though I've said it already, I'll say it one more time because it's that important: Don't ever let something that falls in the Everything Else category trump God and Family. Yes, you have to work and make a living to take care of your family. But to keep your priorities straight, the balance must be weighted in the direction of the first two priorities.

If you are wondering whether your priorities are straight, simply ask your spouse, your children, and those who love you dearly. Make adjustments as necessary. Remember, *it's much more meaningful and rewarding to make a life than to make a living.*

My current reality consists of quite a bit of traveling. However, those traveling events always run through my priority grid. My 9-year-old's piano recital, my 13-year-old's track meet, both of my sons' sporting/school events, family vacations and date nights are more important to me than speaking to thousands of people at a conference. Spending time with your family is more important than working late and overtime hours at your job. Having fun with your family is more important than gathering with your friends.

I remember my publicist sending me an opportunity to appear on a national TV program that reaches millions upon millions of people in over 140 countries. As my assistant and I looked at my schedule, it looked possible that I could make it work with a quick flight in and out of Dallas. But there was one glaring conflict -- my son Wesley's second track meet of the year. He had a great showing at his first meet, and I know it means a lot for his Daddy to be present. I made the decision to turn down this amazing TV opportunity. Both were great alternatives; however, only one of them was the right choice.

A very similar situation happened with my son Jayden's piano recital. Although his portion of the piano recital only lasted a couple of minutes, I would have never had the opportunity to give him a #FistBump and see that big smile on his face when I said 'Well done,' as he nailed his rendition of Bruno Mars' "Grenade."

Sometimes scheduling conflicts will occur; however, when I have the ability to choose... **I will choose to get my priorities straight.**

**"The key is not to prioritize what's on your schedule, but to schedule your priorities." ~ Stephen Covey**

The "To Do or Not To Do" priorities grid (see on next couple pages) has really afforded me the ability to have optimal success in they key areas of my life. Breaking up my to-do's, not to-do's and goals into quarterly segments has really made a big difference. The key to success in this area is having the discipline to not move to the next quarter of "To-Do's and Goals" until those on the previous quarter are complete. This will definitely refine your ability to get things done.

> *"Drive can push, goals can pull and what you let go of lightens the load enough to keep things moving."*
>
> SCOTT WILLIAMS

# To Do Or Not To Do... That is the question.

QTR. 1. TO-DO

QTR. 1. NOT-TO-DO

QTR. 2. TO-DO

QTR. 2. NOT-TO-DO

# To Do Or Not To Do... That is the question.

QTR. 3. TO-DO

QTR. 3. NOT-TO-DO

QTR. 4. TO-DO

QTR. 4. NOT-TO-DO

# Go Deeper Chapter 2 – Three Spheres Of Focus

## GO DREAM

1. How connected are your three spheres? Do they overlap, or do you tend to compartmentalize God, your family and "everything else"?

_____

_____

_____

2. Why do you think it is important to view life in interconnected spheres rather than a linear list of priorities? What does the image imply?

_____

_____

_____

3. Which sphere tends to get the most attention from you? Are you satisfied with this reality or do you need to change some things?

_____

_____

_____

4. Why do you think it is so easy to get distracted when we try too hard to focus on what matters?

_____

_____

_____

# GO DIG

1. Read Matthew 6:33. "But seek first His kingdom and righteousness, and all these things will be given to you as well."

How does this verse make sense when you think about the three spheres?

_____

_____

_____

2. Read Hebrews 11:7a. "By faith Noah, when warned of things not yet seen, in holy fear built an ark to save his family."

How is Noah's life a perfect example of faith, focus and follow through? Are you listening to God first so you know how to lead and love your family?

_____

_____

_____

3. Read Luke 9:61-62. "Still another said, "I will follow you, Lord; but first let me go back and say goodbye to my family." Jesus replied, "No one who puts a hand to the plow and looks back is fit for service in the kingdom of God."

How did this person get the spheres out of order? Do you think Jesus' words were harsh? What does this communicate to you about God's expectations for us?

_____

_____

_____

# GO DO

1. Take some time to complete the "To Do or Not To Do" chart.

**Bonus!** Draw a picture of the three circles and list activities inside of the circles that demonstrate how you are spending your time. What activities demonstrate how you spend time with God, family and everything else? Does your picture look balanced? How can you begin to include God in everything you do?

# NOTES

# NOTES

_____

_____

_____

_____

_____

_____

_____

_____

_____

_____

_____

_____

_____

_____

_____

_____

## ACTION ITEMS

- [ ]
- [ ]
- [ ]
- [ ]

## THOUGHTS

- [ ]
- [ ]
- [ ]
- [ ]

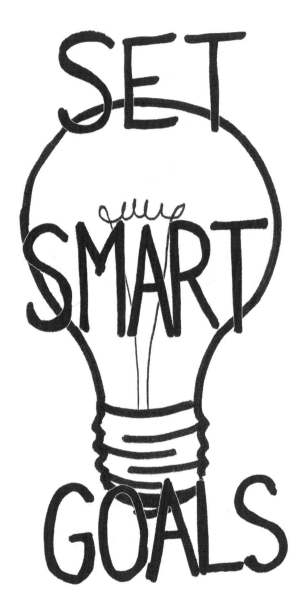

## CHAPTER 3

---

# SET SMART GOALS

---

> *"What you get by achieving your goals is not as important as what you become by achieving your goals."*
>
> ZIG ZIGLAR

I love setting goals. But what I love even more is the feeling of shattering those goals, as I show up and God exceeds my expectations.

As each New Year approaches, many hopeful people look in the mirror and say, "This is going to be the year that [fill-in-the-blank] is going to happen." People crowd into fitness centers, attempt to stop smoking, register for college, seek a better job, attend church on a more regular basis, properly manage their finances… the "Life Improvement List" goes on and on like the Energizer bunny after downing two Five-Hour Energy drinks. All of these changes are great and well-intentioned. The problem is that they don't last.

The adage "The road to hell is paved with good intentions" is definitely applicable when it comes to goal setting. According to research from Proactive Change, nearly 50 percent of American adults will make at least one New Year's resolution, and the majority of these resolutions won't be maintained for more than 30 days. The study also shows that 75 percent of the resolutions will be broken in the first week, and by the end of the year, 97 percent of New Year's resolutions are forgotten.

The problem isn't that people are unwilling to set goals, but that they don't set SMART goals. A successful year requires hard work and a commitment to succeed. Success is one of those things that many want to achieve, but only a few are willing to put in the work necessary to achieve it. Success is a journey. It's a road traveled, and if you want it, you must go after it. If your goal is to succeed (whatever that looks like in your life), you must Go Big and have an unwavering determination.

We have all heard the mottos, quotes and inspirational speeches about success. They all basically say the same thing: If you want to succeed, you have to stop talking about it and be about it. Talk is cheap; hard work pays off. There is no substitute for determination. USA Olympic Gold Medalist and 2012 fan favorite gymnast Gabby Douglass sums it up this way:

*"Gold medals are made of your blood, sweat and tears in the gym." ~Gabby Douglass*

Your life successes are made up of the decisions that you make, coupled with the blood, sweat and tears necessary to keep pressing on toward your goals. Success is about being persistent and aligning your priorities with your dreams and vision for success.

*"Nothing in this world can take the place of persistence. Talent will not; nothing is more common than unsuccessful people with talent. Genius will not; unrewarded genius is almost a proverb. Education will not; the world is full of educated derelicts. Persistence and determination alone are omnipotent. The slogan "press on" has solved and always will solve the problems of the human race." ~ Calvin Coolidge, 30th President of the United States*

There is power in pressing on… Be determined. Press on and set SMART goals.

There are a number of different variations for the acronym SMART.

Some use the words "significant, meaningful, acceptable, realistic, tangible," or other words beneficial to them remembering the acronym. The words I have listed are the most widely used, and the ones that we used during my tenure in the criminal justice field. When I was a prison warden, we used SMART goal setting with both staff and inmates.

The mnemonic SMART has been around for quite some time and was first used in the early 1980s for project management reviews. Again, it doesn't matter what word combination you use. What matters is understanding the hard work, determination and setting of SMART goals that are necessary to be successful.

If you want to ensure a successful year, you must learn how to set SMART goals. The next couple pages will provide a sample SMART Goal Worksheet to help you identify goals and stay on task.

> *"Our goals can only be reached through a vehicle of a plan, in which we must fervently believe, and upon which we must vigorously act. There is no other route to success."*
>
> STEPHEN A. BRENNAN

# Smart Goal Worksheet

## SMART GOAL:

_____

## SPECIFIC –
*Well-defined, clear and unambiguous.*

What do I need to accomplish and why do I need to accomplish it?

_____

_____

_____

## MEASURABLE –
*Able to measure the success and achievement of the goal.*

How much; How many; and How will I know that it's accomplished?

_____

_____

_____

## ATTAINABLE –
*A goal that's aggressive, stretching and within reach.*

How can this goal be accomplished, and is attainment possible?

_____

_____

## RELEVANT -

*A goal that is applicable and relevant to the desired results.*

Does this goal make sense and is it worthwhile?

_____

_____

_____

## TIME-BASED -

*A goal that has a clear timeline & timely target date for completion.*

When? What can I accomplish this week, month, quarter and year?

_____

_____

_____

# Go Deeper Chapter 3 – Set Smart Goals

## GO DREAM

1. A goal is defined as a dream with a deadline. If you don't have a deadline, then you don't have a goal. You just have an idea. How will you turn your ideas into goals?

_____

_____

_____

2. Why do you think most people don't set goals?

_____

_____

_____

3. What current goals are you working on today?

_____

_____

_____

4. On a scale of 1-10, 10 being amazing, how S.M.A.R.T. are your goals?

| 1 | 2 | 3 | 4 | 5 | 6 | 7 | 8 | 9 | 10 |

_____

_____

_____

# GO DIG

1. Read Luke 13:31-33. *"At that time, some Pharisees came to Jesus and said to Him, "Leave this place and go somewhere else. Herod wants to kill you." He relied, "Go tell that fox, 'I will keep on driving out demons and healing people today and tomorrow, and on the third day, I will reach my goal.'"*

_____

_____

_____

How did Jesus demonstrate S.M.A.R.T. goals?

_____

_____

_____

2. Read Philippians 3:14. *"I press on toward the goal to win the prize for which God has called me heavenward in Christ Jesus."*

_____

_____

_____

Are your goals more heavenly or earthly centered?

_____

_____

3. Read 2 Corinthians 5:9. *"So we make it our goal to please Him, whether we are at home in the body or away from it."*

_____

_____

_____

How does your goal of pleasing Jesus show up in your goal setting process?

_____

_____

_____

## GO DO

1. Complete the S.M.A.R.T. goal worksheet.

**Bonus!** Read the book of Nehemiah this week. You can finish it by reading about two chapters a day. It is an incredible story of what it means to take an idea, turn it into a goal and accomplish it for God's glory.

# NOTES

# NOTES

_____

_____

_____

_____

_____

_____

_____

_____

_____

_____

_____

_____

_____

_____

_____

## ACTION ITEMS

- [ ]
- [ ]
- [ ]
- [ ]

## THOUGHTS

- [ ]
- [ ]
- [ ]
- [ ]

# FAST AND PRAY

## CHAPTER 4

# FAST AND PRAY

> *"Prayer honors God, acknowledges His being, exalts His power, adores His providence and secures His aid."*
>
> E.M. BOUNDS

This is where we get down to the nitty-gritty of trying to ensure that you have a successful year.

## FAITH

Although fasting is a spiritual discipline that Jesus encouraged, many Christians are hesitant, confused or unaware when it comes to the biblical principles of fasting. This discipline is important and can have a significant impact on your 3-F's. Not to be the king of alliteration, but it's like adding a 4th F to the equation – Faith, Focus, Follow-Through and Fasting.

Fasting is the practice or discipline of deliberately abstaining from food for one spiritual reason: communication and relationship with the Father. Biblical fasting always occurs together with prayer. You can pray without fasting, but you cannot fast (biblically speaking) without praying. When you are communicating closely with God, your faith and focus will increase.

Prior to 2008, fasting was one of those things I would do periodically for a day or so at a time. My fasting depended on what I was fasting for, or what I felt I was supposed to do. In 2008, I decided to make fasting a part of my yearly spiritual regimen. I read books, committed to fasting and really grew to have an appreciation for the spiritual connection with God during each fast.

In the following years, I began to read and understand more of what fasting is all about. I found that Pastor Jentezen Franklin had some of the best resources on fasting. In fact, I know people who have worked closely with Jentezen, and they've told me that he truly lives, teaches and preaches the fasting lifestyle he so eloquently writes about.

As I began to have a better understanding of fasting, my wife and I both made a commitment to participate in a lengthy "Daniel Fast." Personally, what I like to do is a combination of beginning with 3-7 days of water only and transitioning to the Daniel Fast (vegetables, fruit, whole grains, nuts, legumes, quality oils and water) at the beginning of each year. Our sons participated to a lesser degree, as they had to make some natural adjustments because the groceries in the house were definitely different, and we wanted them to understand the biblical principle of fasting from an early age.

The first year that we truly dedicated the first 21 days of the year to fasting, praying and seeking the Lord, something was unmistakably different in our home life. I can look back and say that it was the kickoff of many spiritual, relational, professional, and family revelations. Every year truly has been better for us since we committed to fasting the first 21 days of each year, as a couple and family.

There have been obvious spiritual connections that occurred during each fast, and I believe there is something about honoring God with the first days of the year that yields amazing fruit in the days and months that follow.

As I talked about in Chapter 1, there is no better way to get your priorities straight than to honor God and to put Him first. If fasting is not a part of your life and walk, I challenge you to make it a discipline. Read the scriptures and seek out resources to learn more about fasting.

If you are looking for immediate direction, I encourage you to buy Jentezen Franklin's books. His first book on the topic, simply called *Fasting*, is a great resource. His more recent release is *The Fasting Edge*. Some of the fasting biblical fasting examples Jentezen gives in his book are:

- **Full Fast** Drink only liquids (you establish the number of days).
- **The Daniel Fast** Eat no meat, no sweets and no bread. Drink water and juice. Eat fruits and vegetables.
- **3-Day Fast** This fast can be a Full Fast, Daniel Fast or fasting from at least one item of food.
- **Partial Fast** A partial fast is from 6 am to 3 pm, or from sun up to sundown. You can select from three types of fasting —a Full Fast, Daniel Fast or give up at least one item of food.
- Scripture References for Fasting: Matthew 6:16-18, Matthew 9:14-15, Luke 18:9-14
- Relation to Prayer and Reading of the Word: 1 Samuel 1:6-8, 17-18, Nehemiah 1:4, Daniel 9:3, 20, Joel 2:12, Luke 2:37, Acts 10:30 ,Acts 13:2
- Corporate Fasting: 1 Samuel 7:5-6, Ezra 8:21-23, Nehemiah 9:1-3, Joel 2:15-16, Jonah 3:5-10, Acts 27:33-37

There is also a corporate 21-day Fast called "Awakening" (awake21. org) that generally kicks off annually the second week of January. Many churches around the country participate in this corporate fast, but you can start a fast any time of the year. An additional web-based resource that many people find helpful is the Daniel Fast Blog - (DanielFast.wordpress.com).

Remember, fasting is not about doing something just to be doing it. It's not just a physical discipline or a religious exercise. If you approach fasting with a pure and sincere heart, and a desire to connect with the Lord on a more intimate level, I believe—and Scripture backs me up-- you'll definitely see extraordinary results.

# PRAY

*"The goal of prayer is the ear of God, a goal that can only be reached by patient and continued and continuous waiting upon Him, pouring out our heart to Him and permitting Him to speak to us. Only by so doing can we expect to know Him, and as we come to know Him better we shall spend more time in His presence and find that presence a constant and ever-increasing delight." ~ E.M. Bounds*

Prayer is an essential part of the Christian walk, but unfortunately it's something that gets lost for many of us in the daily occurrences of life. Just as praying can easily be neglected, it's also a discipline that we can easily grow in each day. Not only does God deserve this time with you, but it will also have a powerfully positive effect on that goal of a successful year.

For many people, prayer is difficult. They don't know what to say and how to say it. Research shows that one of the greatest fears people have is speaking in public. Praying in public takes that fear and magnifies it. It's almost like people think they're praying in front of the judges on "Prayerican Idol." As if Randy Jackson is going to say, "Yo Dawg, for me for you that wasn't your best prayer. It was kinda pitchy in spots. Not sure it's good enough to reach God." Obviously, that's not the case at all. Prayer is having an "ordinary" conversation; what makes it extraordinary is that you're having it with God. It can take place in whatever shape, form or fashion. It's simply about acknowledging His power and being thankful that you can secure His help.

## AN HOUR A DAY KEEPS THE DOCTOR AWAY

A practical way to connect with God is to devote at least an hour each day to prayer. An hour may sound like a long time at first, but it's easier than you think.

- ☾ **15 Minutes in the morning:** Wake up early to pray, read your Bible and pray some more. Start your day off right and go to God for your daily bread. This is a great time for couples to pray together daily.
- ☽ **15 Minutes at lunch:** I'm not talking about praying a continuous 15-minute prayer before your meal. Simply take a few minutes prior to leaving for lunch, a few during lunch, and a few on your drive to and from lunch. The time and connection will quickly add up.
- ➔ **15 Minutes at the end of business:** The end of business varies from person to person; I'm referring to the time of day that you stop professional tasks and transition into personal time (for some, that time is 5 p.m.). Take 15 minutes before you leave from work or 15 minutes on your drive home to talk with God before the distractions of home take over.
- ➔ **15 Minutes before bedtime:** This is a great time to incorporate family prayer, couples prayer, or praying with the kids before you go to bed.

**Disclaimer:** Praying during drive time should be with your eyes open and on the road. Just like you shouldn't drink and drive, or text and drive, you shouldn't pray with your eyes closed and drive. You may be able to walk by faith and not by sight, but that doesn't apply to driving.

Although this one hour each day is a minimal amount of time, it's vitally important. Allocating that time helps us to get into the discipline of having ongoing conversation and connection with God. It is also the time that we can seek His aid for guidance, wisdom, focus, clarity, healing, freedom and strength.

Regular prayer time with your family also has the benefit of drawing you closer together. When it comes to prayer, relationships and marriage, we've all heard the old adage that "couples who pray together stay together." The research from Dr. Tom Ellis, chairman of the Southern Baptist Convention's Council on The Family, showed that "born-again Christian couples who marry after receiving premarital counseling, attend church together regularly, and pray together daily have a less than 1 percent divorce rate." I know that statistic sounds crazy because the statistic that we all know is that roughly 50 percent of both Christian and non-Christian marriages end in a divorce. The key to the research is "pray together daily." Most couples don't pray together daily and when they do, they learn to take things to God on a daily basis. They demonstrate the priority of letting go and letting God.

Make prayer a priority, and set goals for spending time in prayer. It is a surefire way to have a year of success.

> "To be a Christian without prayer is no more possible than to be alive without breathing."
>
> MARTIN LUTHER KING JR.

## GO DREAM

1. What adjustments would you have to make in our life if you committed to regular fasting? How do you think it would change your focus?

_____

_____

_____

2. Why do you think fasting is so difficult for people to do?

_____

_____

_____

3. We are asked to "pray without ceasing." How is this practical? What does this communicate about your posture before God?

_____

_____

_____

4. Why do you think it is pointless to fast and not pray? Why should the two be done together?

_____

_____

_____

# GO DIG

1. Read Matthew 6:16-18. *"When you fast, do not look somber as the hypocrites do, for they disfigure their faces to show others they are fasting. Truly I tell you, they have received their reward in full. But when you fast, put oil on your head and wash your face, so that it will not be obvious to others that you are fasting, but only to your Father, who is unseen; and your Father, who sees what is done in secret, will reward you."*

Jesus said "when" you fast, not "if" you fast. In other words, He expects it of His followers. Are you living up to His expectations?

_____

_____

_____

2. Read Acts 13:2. *"While they were worshiping the Lord and fasting, the Holy Spirit said, "Set apart for me Barnabas and Saul for the work to which I have called them."*

How does this verse communicate that when we fast, God acts? What are you waiting on God to do? Would fasting help connect your heart with God's heart?

_____

_____

_____

3. Read Acts 27:33-37. *"Just before dawn Paul urged them all to eat. "For the last fourteen days," he said, "you have been in constant suspense and have gone without food—you haven't eaten anything. Now I urge you to take some food. You need it to survive. Not one of you will lose a single hair from his head." After He said this, He took some bread and gave thanks to God in front of them all. Then He*

*broke it and began to eat. They were all encouraged and ate some food themselves. Altogether, there were 276 of us on board."*

Much like exercise, it is easier to fast with people encouraging you and holding you accountable. Who can you ask to fast with you? What do you think that would do for your friendships?

_____

_____

_____

## GO DO

1. What do you want God to accomplish in your life? Many believers tend to seek God's hands before they are willing to seek His heart. Are you willing to seek God's heart and hands in every area of your life?

_____

_____

_____

2. Commit to praying for 1 hour a day as suggested in the 15-minute segments.

3. Pick a type of fast and ask at least one person to join you and see what God will do through it.

**Bonus!** Journal about your experience as you learn what it means to fast and pray.

# NOTES

# NOTES

---
---
---
---
---
---
---
---
---
---
---
---
---
---
---
---
---
---
---
---

## ACTION ITEMS

- [ ]
- [ ]
- [ ]
- [ ]

## THOUGHTS

- [ ]
- [ ]
- [ ]
- [ ]

# SIMPLIFY
# LESS IS MORE

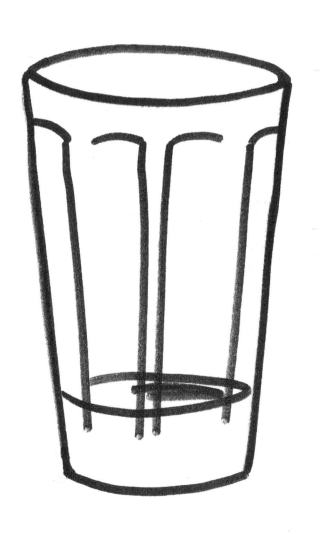

## CHAPTER 5

## SIMPLIFY - LESS IS MORE

> *"Simplicity is the ultimate form of sophistication."*
>
> LEONARDO DA VINCI

A s a leader, I learned early on the importance of simplicity. When I was a prison warden over a decade ago, I remember having regular meetings with my key staff, to discuss what could be done to simplify their job and to encourage them to stop trying so hard.

The answers to the simplicity question were usually practical things, such as minimizing paperwork, reducing bureaucratic logjams, and streamlining of central office vs. prison facility relationships/processes. While we were able to make some headway on the simplicity concept, it seemed to take more time for some to understand the concept of "not trying so hard."

Often, the staff felt as though the inmates would respond better if they were over-the-top, or their supervisors would notice them if they tried really hard. They had to learn the difference between being a hard-working, rule-following type of employee, and an employee that simply tried way too hard. The reality was that the employees that tried way too hard were the ones that caused most of the problems in our prison facility, because they were too focused on what the inmates and their supervisor thought of them. They needed to appear hard to the inmates and appear hardworking to their supervisor.

I've always valued a culture of simplicity and not trying so hard. I also value a culture of high performance. Although people may think the two are mutually exclusive, high performance and lack of over-trying go hand in hand. With high performance and doing what's right, the right way will begin to come naturally.

When the leader falls into the "Trying Too Hard" category, it creates problems for everyone. Relax, chill and stop trying so hard! The people that you are trying to impress can see right through that mess. Focus on creating a culture of simplicity. Let the extraordinary naturally unfold from the ordinary moments of faithful effort.

Some ways that you as a leader can create a culture of simplicity instead of a culture of "Trying Too Hard" may include:

- Relax and stop making everything a "Big Deal." Don't take yourself, others or situations so seriously.
- Give "over-the-top" employees constructive criticism and open feedback to help them identify the areas where they can maybe tone it down.
- Avoid knee-jerk reactions.
- Embrace the "5 Minute / 5 Phone Calls" concept. – There is nothing that we can't begin the process of fixing in five minutes or five phone calls.
- Outline clear expectations and expect things to be executed. (Follow up; don't follow around. See next bullet point.)
- Allow your team to have some space and do their jobs without you breathing all over them. (Avoid micromanagement.)
- Realize that meetings don't make you better. (Minimize meeting times, the number of meetings, and who needs to be present – free your people.)
- Reduce the amount of paperwork, steps, hoops, processes, etc.

- Create a culture of healthy conflict and minimize drama. One of my favorite R&B artists, Mary J. Blige, has an album called *No More Drama* – that should be the title track for a new culture of simplicity.

## LESS IS MORE

"Less is more" is about working smart instead of working hard. "Less is more" means embracing and understanding the fundamental difference between being active and being productive. Over the years, I have worked with many different types of people as an employee, supervisor, and co-worker. I have seen that unfortunately, too many people confuse activity for productivity. They're two very different animals. If you want to ensure a year of success, you will have to function in the realm of productivity, and move out of the realm of mere activity. Take a look at these brief definitions of the two:

- **Activity-** The state or quality of being active.
- **Productivity-** The efficiency with which work or output is produced.

Just because a person, group, or team is active, doesn't necessarily mean that they are efficient or productive. This applies to both personal and business life. When individuals presume that **Activity = Productivity**, they create a system in which their primary goal is to be active. They will work long hours, always try to look busy, and encourage those around them to keep busy. Each day they tell themselves, "I have lots of stuff to work on today, and I need to get busy." Their mindset of busyness often proves to impede productivity, due to the fact that their primary focus is simply to be active.

The productive person, on the other hand, will ask themselves these types of questions: "What do I need to work on today?" "Am I working on the things that matter?" "What do I need to put on my not-to-do list?" "How can I become more efficient?"

Again, these same concepts of simplicity move beyond our work life into our personal lives. We must consistently ask ourselves what are we doing to simplify our lives at home and demonstrate to our families that we truly believe in the ideals of "Less is More."

I mentioned the Not-To-Do List in Chapter 2. The not-to-do list is important because when people are "Going Big" they will spend a lot of time filling up their To-Do List. In the process of driving towards results, it's equally as important to have a **Not To-Do List**. This list should be filled with things that you simply are not going to do. There are things that you will have to give up in order to go up.

If you want to have a successful year, you must give up some things. Get rid of the unnecessary so that you may truly embrace the necessary. I have found a "sweet spot" between where the to-do lists and not-to-do lists overlap. I call this the "Go Zone." Finding the "Go Zone" leads to finding the "Grow Zone."

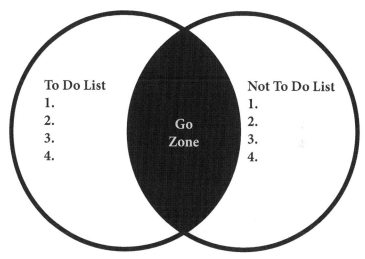

Don't be surprised when there is tension between the to-do and not-to-do. Some things will collide with one another; the friction that happens between what you want to do and what you need to give up will create some positive momentum. Change is movement, and movement creates friction. That tension is a good sign! There is no movement without friction.

Although you are focused on simplicity, you should also be willing to try something new, start a new adventure, or take a new risk. Believe it or not, the act of trying new things and taking new calculated risks will help you to ascertain how you can truly simplify. Planting new seeds provides an understanding of the types of seeds you desire to sow and the types of soil in which they can germinate. The process of elimination always contributes to a more sophisticated process of simplification. Although this may sound conflicted, trying something new contributes to the idea of "Less is more!" Replacing clunky old systems with simplified new ones nearly always pulls extraordinary results out of ordinary procedures.

*"Simple can be harder than complex: You have to work hard to get your thinking clean to make it simple. But it's worth it in the end because once you get there, you can move mountains."*

STEVE JOBS

# Go Deeper Chapter 5 - Simplify - Less Is More

## GO DREAM

1. Would you categorize your life as simple or complex?

_____

_____

_____

2. What kind of things demonstrate that a person is living a simple life? Complex life?

_____

_____

_____

3. Why do you think it is so complex to simplify?

_____

_____

_____

4. If you could reduce your life down to FIVE responsibilities, which ones would make your top FIVE?

1. _____

2. _____

3. _____

4. _____

5. _____

# GO DIG

1. Read Matthew 13:55a. *"Isn't this the carpenter's son?"*

Jesus was the most complex God-man that has ever walked the face of the earth, yet He lived a simple life. What can we learn from our Leader?

_____

_____

_____

2. Read Matthew 11:28-30. *"Come to me, all you who are weary and burdened, and I will give you rest. Take my yoke upon you and learn from me, for I am gentle and humble in heart, and you will find rest for your souls. For my yoke is easy and my burden is light."*

If your life is complex, heavy and burdened, then you are carrying the wrong load. How will living a life with Jesus provide you with rest, simplicity and ease?

_____

_____

_____

3. Read Matthew 23:24. *"You blind guides! You strain out a gnat but swallow a camel."*

These were the words of Jesus to religious hypocrites that complicated life. What are some practical ways that you can begin to focus on the right parts of your story/life? How can you simplify your life?

_____

_____

_____

# GO DO

1. Take this week and really take some steps to simplify how you live your life. It may mean stopping certain activities. It may mean selling unnecessary things. It may mean calling a few people for advice. Make the commitment to do what is necessary to eliminate the unnecessary.

**Bonus!** Simplicity Ideas:

- Spend a day in your underwear or Pajamas just to remind yourself that we really don't need much. (Side note: Wait for a day when no one else is home. It will be better for all involved.)
- Spend a day without your cell phone.
- Spend an afternoon walking a trail.
- Spend a day or week free from technology.
- Spend one week eating Ramen noodles every way you can imagine. (There are entire Ramen noodle cookbooks out there.)

# NOTES

# NOTES

_____
_____
_____
_____
_____
_____
_____
_____
_____
_____
_____
_____
_____
_____
_____
_____
_____

## ACTION ITEMS

- [ ]
- [ ]
- [ ]
- [ ]

## THOUGHTS

- [ ]
- [ ]
- [ ]
- [ ]

## CHAPTER 6

## HELP OTHERS WIN

> *"How can I help others win?" is the most pressing question that a leader must ask themselves."*
>
> SCOTT WILLIAMS

Finding your life's purpose and calling is such a rewarding experience. It's that moment you realize, "*This* is what I'm about. *This* is one of the things I was created to do. *This* is what makes me tick. *This* is what I'm passionate about. *This* is me!"

Over the years, I have always heard from others what they thought I was all about -- that I was created to encourage, inspire and help others. It wasn't until I had the crystal-clear visualization from God that it was confirmed for me. It was that "ah ha!" moment when I said, "God created me to help others win!"

Ever since I can remember, my focus has been answering the question of what I can do to make those around me better. That's the core purpose for me writing this very book. God put me here to help others win.

Over the years, I have found that **Helping Others Win** is a very important duty for everyone. As leaders, our primary goal is to help those we lead win. As followers, our primary goal is to help those we follow win. If we are winning, and those around us are winning, then our organization wins. That's a win-win-win situation.

As parents, it's important to help our children win. We provide environments, teaching, structure, systems, beliefs and assistance that help create opportunities for success. As married couples, we must be wholly committed to helping our spouse win.

**Helping Others Win** is such a simple concept, but it's often overlooked in this self-consumed age. It's much easier for a boss to fire someone, a coach to give up on someone, and a spouse to hit the road than it is to commit to helping another person win.

Actor Charlie Sheen may be more than a little off of his rocker, but the one thing he seems to get is how great it is to be Winning. In one of Sheen's crazed rants about people thinking that he's a mental case, Sheen was quoted as saying "I'm not bi-polar, I'm bi-winning." I'm not sure what his intent was with that statement. But I think the concept is brilliant.

We all need to become more focused on being bi-winning -- creating situations where everyone wins. Do you want to ensure a successful tomorrow? Go Big by helping someone win today.

## WINNING AND WIELDING INFLUENCE

Some of the greatest winners of our time helped others win. Michael Jordan is unquestionably the best basketball player to ever step on the hardwood. One of the great things about Jordan was the fact that he helped those around him elevate their game. You can look at Kukoc, Kerr, Rodman, Pippen, Paxson, Grant, and many others to see how Jordan had a commitment to helping others win.

#Tebowed – (verb) another word for #winning. A more modern athlete is the highly polarizing Tim Tebow. Tim is all about helping others win by encouraging, challenging, and inspiring them to be better. The only way that this happens is if the leader is willing to lead by example and has a commitment to get better.

The sign of a great "helping others win" leader is someone who inspires those around them to greatness. In seven out of nine of Tim Tebow's first starts as the Broncos QB, in my opinion he inspired the Broncos defense to be better. You are kidding yourself if you don't think the Broncos defense got fired up to know that they have a chance to win if they can just keep their team close.

You are kidding yourself if you don't think that Broncos Hall-Of-Famer and Executive Vice President of Football Operations John Elway learned a thing or two about helping others win, leadership, and faith from Tebow.

Not only did the Broncos always have a chance to win, they were bi-winning thanks to the Tebow persona. I was talking to a friend that lives in Denver, and he made mention that Tebow inspired down-and-out fans, business owners, educators, the entire city of Denver. Due to the fact that he was literally the sole iconic figure in Denver, and for that matter the state of Colorado, he galvanized the Mile High City, inspiring residents to believe they can accomplish things that may seem a "mile high."

Sports fan or not, 2011 allowed everyone to see an amazing story unfold each Sunday with Tebow's winning attitude. I loved watching the trends on Twitter during and after a Broncos game. Not everyone is a fan; however, in the eight consecutive weeks that I conducted the "Tim Tebow" Twitter search, I saw a trend develop.

Not only did I see more and more people becoming believers in Tim Tebow's abilities as a QB, I saw more and more people who appeared to have no prior belief in God begin to have some belief, or at least start to ask questions. The miraculous nature of Tebow's play and the Broncos' comebacks had people in the world of Twitter making statements like: *"Tim Tebow makes me want to believe what he believes," "Tim Tebow is proof that God is real," "Not gonna lie I don't believe most preachers, but this Tim Tebow kid makes me want 2 go back 2 church," "Tim Tebow = Touchdown Jesus."* Many are too inappropriate to share; nonetheless, they point toward questions of God, faith and football.

You have to take what people on Twitter are saying with a grain of salt; however, you can't dismiss the fact that Tebow is making a Kingdom of God impact. After one of the heroic Bronco wins, Tebow began his post-game press conference with his usual, *"First and foremost I'd like to thank my Lord and savior, Jesus Christ, and after that I just want to thank my teammates and coaches."* Tebow went on to say, *"If you believe, unbelievable things can sometimes be possible."* With **Faith, Focus and Follow-Through** extraordinary things can happen.

## COMPETITIVE GREATNESS

One thing we can learn from Tebow about helping others win is something that he learned from Urban Meyer, his coach at the University of Florida, and from Broncos coach John Fox. Meyer calls it "competitive excellence" and Fox calls it "competitive greatness." No matter what you call it, Tebow and the Broncos exemplified it. In Tebow's words, **competitive greatness** means: *"When your number's called in the clutch time, you better step up and make the play."*

You have to be willing, able and ready for competitive greatness to happen. If you help others win, believe in others and encourage others, they will be more than ready to step up when their number is called.

Remember that helping others win is not about you, but others. Tebow puts it into perspective with this statement about why he is so forward about sharing his faith. *"If someone asks, I'll always be willing to share His will because I also know that there are a lot more important things than football and that is one of them. That ultimately overrides football any day of the week. It's just a game; it's a game that we are passionate about. It's more important for me to use my platform to honor God and influence kids in a positive way."* In other words, it's not about me; it's about helping others win.

Tebow's weekly performances were not always great, and their season ended a mile low, according to many. Tim Tebow's future with the Broncos ended with the team's acquisition of Peyton Manning, arguably one of the best quarterbacks to ever play the game. Tebow was traded to the New York Jets, and his future is still up in the air, or rather up in the Big Apple. After only a short time of Tebow being in Jets Camp, Jets all-pro cornerback and straight shooter Darrelle Revis was quoted as saying this about Tebow, *"He's a born leader, very few athletes have the gift that he has. He tries to lead by example all the time and he tries to be positive. Some people have it. Some guys don't. It's the passion within… of him wanting to be a leader, wanting to win. You see it in him all the time, he's just one of those guys, he's very positive. He has passion for what he does and you could see it. You can see it on him when you have a conversation with him. He's just a leader."*

No matter what happens, Tebow's willingness to make a positive impact on those influenced by his platform has and will always be great.

There are many different illustrations, examples, and thoughts that demonstrate the importance and value of helping others win. If you want to ensure a successful year, make sure you are focused on developing others and helping others win.

## LEADERSHIP DEVELOPMENT IS THE HIGHEST CALLING OF LEADERSHIP

Leadership development is one of the ultimate forms of helping others win, because it's winning that keeps on winning. It duplicates itself over and over. Unfortunately, leadership development is one of those terms that people throw around with ease, often without embracing the true essence of what it's all about. The reality is that leadership development is one of the ultimate callings of leadership. Without leadership development, you won't reproduce more leaders.

Leadership development requires a leader to focus on the success of those they lead, while simultaneously focusing on the vision of the organization. It's about helping others win. Those things can happen simultaneously and are not mutually exclusive.

When leaders have a genuine interest in and commitment to making sure that those they lead are successful, that's true leadership development. It requires varied approaches, pushing through struggles, and recognition that if individual team members win in their respective roles, the team wins overall.

Leadership development takes time, energy and focus. It takes putting your arm around a team member, child or friend and helping them to win. Often, leaders confuse leadership development with an event, program or formula. Events and programs are only minor components in a successful leadership development equation. Genuine care, concern, and individualized focus on team members' success trumps a program, event, or leadership development "lip service" every time. If you want to know more and understand the complexities and benefits of genuine leadership development, you should read *The Leadership Engine – How Winning Companies Build Leaders at Every Level* by Noel Tichy. This book has been around for many years and is the fundamental guidebook when it comes to leadership development.

Genuine leadership development always inspires a deep inner desire for self-development. Talk about a win-win situation. The leader genuinely cares about the development of team members; moreover, the team members are inspired to care more acutely about their own development. When everyone identifies their personal success with the group's success, extraordinary results are guaranteed.

Leadership is more than a title, position or a corner office. It's about propelling the vision of the organization that you're leading while simultaneously helping others win. Remember that it's always easier to get rid of someone than it is to take the time to develop them. It's easier to tell that prodigal son or daughter it's time for them to go than it is to develop them to be a winner. Leadership is always about making the right decision, and a swift decision to fire someone without investing time in genuine development is often not the right decision.

If you look at Jesus and His disciples, He kept the vision in focus while simultaneously putting his arm around His disciples and developing them over time. Development takes time.

I appreciate the view of the founder of Firestone Tires. Harvey Firestone sums up the call of leadership by saying, *"The growth and development of people is the highest calling of leadership."* Harvey Firestone makes tires, and understands that adding leadership tread to others is the process of helping others win.

## ENCOURAGING, DEVELOPING AND MENTORING

**Be a Barnabas to Others** -- Barnabas was the son of encouragement. He was always looking for someone to encourage, and encouragement was simply his nature. As followers of Christ, it's important that we be an encouragement to those around us. People tend to become what the most important people in their life thinks they will become. Encourage someone today; **be a Barnabas!**

**Seek Out a Paul.** If we want to help others win, we must understand the process of being mentored and the process of mentoring, It's important that we all seek out that Paul to pour into our lives. This mentoring relationship can begin with observing individuals with qualities that you would like to see instilled within yourself. The initial mentoring relationship can occur from afar, simply by observing. At some point it's important for the individual who's seeking out their Paul to ask that person to be their mentor. I have had people ask me directly, "Will you be a Paul in my life." After "The Ask" has occurred, it's important to sit down and line out expectations for the mentoring relationship. **Seek Out a Paul!**

**Pour Into a Timothy.** Just as Paul trained up, poured into and developed Timothy, it's important for each of us, especially leaders, to find a Timothy to pour into. **Pour Into a Timothy!**

People development is the ultimate form of helping others win, and helping others win is the ultimate form of winning.

"A good objective of leadership is to help those who are doing poorly to do well and to help those who are doing well to do even better."

JIM ROHN

## GO DREAM

1. How good are you at helping others win?

2. How good would others say you are at helping them win? Is what you think and what others say consistent?

3. Helping others win means that you are serving them. How does serving others inspire them to reach their potential?

4. If you could help one person in your life win, who would it be? What would be your first steps?

# GO DIG

1. Read Matthew 23:11. *"The greatest among you will be your servant."*

How does this verse apply to helping others win? How does this make you a winner in the eyes of Jesus?

_____

_____

_____

2. Read Luke 10:30-37. *"In reply Jesus said: "A man was going down from Jerusalem to Jericho, when he was attacked by robbers. They stripped him of his clothes, beat him and went away, leaving him half dead. A priest happened to be going down the same road, and when he saw the man, he passed by on the other side. So too, a Levite, when he came to the place and saw him, passed by on the other side. But a Samaritan, as he traveled, came where the man was; and when he saw him, he took pity on him. He went to him and bandaged his wounds, pouring on oil and wine. Then he put the man on his own donkey, brought him to an inn and took care of him. The next day he took out two denarii and gave them to the innkeeper. 'Look after him,' he said, 'and when I return, I will reimburse you for any extra expense you may have. ""Which of these three do you think was a neighbor to the man who fell into the hands of robbers?" The expert in the law replied, "The one who had mercy on him." Jesus told him, "Go and do likewise."*

It is clear a group of robbers did not want their victim to win, and the Samaritan man went out of his way to make sure the man was set up to win. Is it possible that we rob people of their potential when we don't step in to help? Who can you set up today to win?

_____

_____

_____

3. Read Mark 2:1-5. *"A few days later, when Jesus again entered Capernaum, the people heard that He had come home. They gathered in such large numbers that there was no room left, not even outside the door, and He preached the Word to them. Some men came, bringing to Him a paralyzed man, carried by four of them. Since they could not get him to Jesus because of the crowd, they made an opening in the roof above Jesus by digging through it and then lowered the mat the man was lying on. When Jesus saw their faith, He said to the paralyzed man, "Son, your sins are forgiven."*

The best way to help people win is to introduce them to the person responsible for you winning – Jesus Christ. What excuses have you used to not help others? Are you willing to do whatever it takes to see people win?

_____

_____

# GO DO

1. Identify at least one person that you can partner with to help them win. Who can you mentor? Who can you pour into? Who can you serve? What practical things will you do to start the journey and see it to its completion?

_____

_____

**Bonus!** Make a list of five people that you plan to help win this year. Begin to pray for them and see what God does.

1. _____

2. _____

3. _____

4. _____

5. _____

# NOTES

# NOTES

_____

_____

_____

_____

_____

_____

_____

_____

_____

_____

_____

_____

_____

_____

_____

## ACTION ITEMS

- [ ]
- [ ]
- [ ]
- [ ]

## THOUGHTS

- [ ]
- [ ]
- [ ]
- [ ]

# ERA

CHAPTER 7

---

## ERA

---

> *"The pessimist complains about the wind; the optimist expects it to change; the realist adjusts the sails."*

WILLIAM ARTHUR WARD

**W**hen you see the letters ERA, what do you think of? For some of you, you're thinking of a period of time marked with distinctive character, or the beginning and ending of a specific set of years. Others of you may be thinking about your favorite Major League Baseball pitcher with the lowest Earned Run Average. Those of you with a little more historical knowledge may be thinking of The Equal Rights Amendment Act.

As we look at taking our lives from ordinary to extraordinary, ERA refers to **Evaluate > Reevaluate > Action.**

- **Evaluate** – You must give an accurate evaluation of where you have been, where you are, and where you are going. Give those closest to you permission to speak candidly into your life. Ups, downs, successes, failures, and areas in which you have gotten off track. This is where you ask the tough questions and embrace the tough answers. Do I have my priorities straight (God, then family, then everything else)?

Did I set SMART goals? How am I tracking on my goals? Am I making fasting a part of my spiritual disciplines? Am I consistently taking the time to pray? Am I praying at least an hour each day? Am I truly seeking the Lord? How am I simplifying my life? Am I helping others win?

- **Reevaluate** – Once you authentically evaluate where you have been, where you are, and where you are going, it's time to reevaluate. You can't stop with asking the tough questions and taking a snapshot of your progress. You must take the next step and re-visit the areas where you have identified blind spots, failures, and limited success. Additionally, you must look at the areas that are firing on all cylinders. During this re-evaluate stage, you must go to those individuals who gave you feedback in the Evaluate stage and ask them to press a little harder, go a little deeper, and flesh out more details. This re-evaluate process allows you to take a second look in the mirror and check your side mirrors, and ultimately sets you up for success.

- **Action** – Take all the information that you have evaluated and put it into action – Do Something About It. This process is ongoing, as you will always be evaluating, re-evaluating and putting pertinent discoveries into action. ERA is the most important step to ensure continuous success.

*"Your life is the sum of your choices... Choose Wisely!"*

In life, you may not be able to change the direction of the winds, but you can adjust your sails to reach your destination. A great captain makes necessary adjustments to their course. You must be willing to make course corrections if you want to succeed. If you want to ensure a successful year, you must keep your eyes, mind, and heart open to receiving candid feedback and a willingness to make course corrections. If you stand ready to learn, opportunities to be taught will be all around you.

*"Success is not a destination city... it's an everlasting highway."*

This is going to be a year of success because you are Going Big and you are committed to winning. Rise up, grab the bull by the horns, and claim a year of success. If showing up is half of the battle, showing up with a plan and following through on that plan is the other half. You have a plan, you are committed to showing up, you are getting off the sidelines, getting in the game and winning.

Theologian Williams Shedd says it this way, *"A ship is safe at harbor, but that's not what ships are for."* The same is true for you. You are safe on the sidelines, you are safe doing more of the same, you are safe settling for "what is" rather than searching for "what could be", you are safe settling – but that's not what you were made for. You were made to Go BIG.

*Seize life! Eat bread with gusto, Drink wine with a robust heart. Oh yes-God takes pleasure in your pleasure! Dress festively every morning. Don't skimp on colors and scarves. Relish life with the spouse you love Each and every day of your precarious life. Each day is God's gift. It's all you get in exchange For the hard work of staying alive. Make the most of each one! Whatever turns up, grab it and do it. And heartily! This is your last and only chance at it, For there's neither work to do nor thoughts to think In the company of the dead, where you're most certainly headed.* ~ Ecclesiastes 9:7-11 MSG

Each day is God's gift. Open your gift, steward your gift, seize life and Go BIG. If you choose to Go BIG, where you're going will be extraordinarily better than where you've been.

Cheers to an extraordinary future!

# Go Deeper Chapter 7 – ERA

## GO DREAM

1. Which is the most difficult part of the ERA for you? Evaluate? Re-Evaluate? Action?

_____

_____

_____

2. How can you begin to improve your ERA?

_____

_____

_____

3. How do you need to adjust your sails to reach your destination?

_____

_____

_____

_____

4. Are you tired of being on the sidelines? Are you bored with the shore? What is your first step to take your life from Ordinary to Extraordinary?

_____

_____

_____

# GO DIG

1. Read Luke 14:28. *"Suppose one of you wants to build a tower. Won't you first sit down and estimate the cost to see if you have enough money to complete it?"*

It is so easy to start something and so difficult to finish. Have you sat down to evaluate if you have what it takes? Are you trusting yourself or are you trusting in your God?

_____

_____

_____

2. Read Proverbs 13:25. *"Ants are creatures of little strength, yet they store up their food in the summer."*

How are you planning to succeed this year? Why is planning so critical to improving your ERA?

_____

_____

_____

3. Read Psalm 20:4. *"May He give you the desire of your heart and make all your plans succeed."*

If your desire is God's desire, then you will succeed. What are some practical things that you can do to ensure that you desire what God desires?

_____

_____

_____

_____

# GO DO

1. Spend some time doing the ERA. Evaluate your life. Re-evaluate just to make sure that your assessment of reality is correct. Take action! Write down your evaluation, re-evaluation and your action steps. Put it in a place where you can see it on a regular basis. Pray for change. Pray for growth. Pray that you have the biggest year of your life!

**Bonus:** Read Matthew 5-7. These three chapters are commonly referred to as the Sermon on the Mount. This is Jesus' idea for how life works and since He is Life, it is always the best idea to learn from Him. Journal about what you learn and share it with those around you.

# NOTES

# Notes

---

---

---

---

---

---

---

---

---

---

---

---

---

---

---

---

---

---

## Action Items

- [ ]
- [ ]
- [ ]
- [ ]

## Thoughts

- [ ]
- [ ]
- [ ]
- [ ]

## PARABLE OF THE DUCKS

---

## **FINAL THOUGHT**

---

'll close with a paraphrase of one of my favorite illustrations from the great 19th century Danish philosopher Søren Kierkegaard's famous Parable of the Ducks. In it, Kierkegaard describes a great town where only ducks live.

## PARABLE OF THE DUCKS

… One Sunday morning, the ducks waddled out of their houses and down to their church. They waddled through the doors and squatted comfortably in the pews.

The duck choir sang, and the duck congregation sang along. Finally, the duck pastor came to proclaim the message. He opened his duck bible and eloquently delivered a powerful sermon.

Then he encouraged the congregation, "Ducks, God has given you wings! With these wings, you can fly!" he said.

"With these wings, you can rise up and soar like eagles! No walls can confine you, no fences can hold you. You have wings, and you can fly like birds!"

All the ducks shouted, "We can fly, we can fly!"

The duck pastor encouraged them again, "You can fly ducks, you can soar like eagles."

Again, the ducks yelled, "We can fly, we can soar." The entire duck congregation shouted, "Amen!"

With that, the pastor closed his duck bible and dismissed the congregation of ducks.

All of the ducks left the service, commenting on what a life-changing message they had just heard.

And they all waddled back to their houses.


You weren't born to live an ordinary life. You've been given unique gifts, abilities, untapped potential, intellect, passions and dreams so that you can live an extraordinary life.

Don't acknowledge that you have the God-given potential to fly and then simply choose to waddle! Don't go small. Go BIG!

# REFERENCES

ThinkExist.com Quotations Copyright ® ThinkExist 1999-2012

Dictionary.com, LLC Copyright © 2012 All rights reserved.

Proactive Change is a Registered Service Mark of Serge Prengel. (C) 2012

New International Version®, NIV®. Copyright ©1973, 1978, 1984, 2011 by Biblica, Inc.™ Used by permission of Zondervan. All rights reserved worldwide.

The Message by Eugene H. Peterson, copyright © 1993, 1994, 1995, 1996, 2000, 2001, 2002. Used by permission of NavPress Publishing Group. All Rights Reserved.

http://todayinlondonblog.today.com/ © 2012 NBCNews.com

ReligiousTolerance.org, Dr. Tom Ellis Copyright © 2000 to 2009 by Ontario Consultants on Religious Tolerance

The leadership engine: How winning companies build leaders at every level, by Noel M. Tichy. (1997). New York: HarperBusiness

Fasting - Opening the door to a deeper, more intimate, more powerful relationship with God, Jentezen Franklin. (2007) Charisma House.

# CONNECT WITH AUTHOR SCOTT WILLIAMS

**TWITTER**
@ScottWilliams

**FACEBOOK**
facebook.com/scottwilliams.tv

**BLOG**
www.BigIsTheNewSmall.com

**THE BOOK**
www.GoBigBook.com